Hei
~

(loud
through
house)

To:

Mandy

♡

From:

Jessica

Date:

_2023_

Hospice store when the ♡
"BAG" of books is
$1.00

Amazing Love

Celebrating the True Meaning of Easter

Pi Pocket
INSPIRATIONS

summerside
PRESS

© 2012 Summerside Press™
Minneapolis, MN 55337
www.summersidepress.com

Amazing Love

Celebrating the True Meaning of Easter
A *Pocket Inspirations* Book

ISBN 978-1-60936-599-8

Scripture references are from the following sources: The Holy Bible, New
International Version®, NIV®. Copyright © 1973, 1978, 1984, 2011 by Biblica,
Inc.™ Used by permission of Zondervan. All rights reserved worldwide.
(Scripture quotations marked NIV† are taken from the NIV® 1984 version.)
The New King James Version (NKJV). Copyright © 1982 by Thomas Nelson,
Inc. Used by permission. The Holy Bible, English Standard Version® (ESV),
copyright © 2001 by Crossway Bibles, a publishing ministry of Good News
Publishers. Used by permission. The New American Standard Bible® (NASB),
Copyright © 1960, 1962, 1963, 1968, 1971, 1972, 1973, 1975, 1977, 1995 by
The Lockman Foundation. Used by permission. The Holy Bible, New Living
Translation (NLT), copyright 1996, 2004, 2007 by Tyndale House Foundation.
Used by permission of Tyndale House Publishers, Inc., Carol Stream, Illinois
60188. The Message (MSG). Copyright © 1993, 1994, 1995, 1996, 2000, 2001,
2002 by Eugene Peterson. Used by permission of NavPress, Colorado Springs,
CO. All rights reserved.

Excluding Scripture verses and divine pronouns, in some quotations
references to men and masculine pronouns have been replaced with gender-
neutral or feminine references. Additionally, in some quotations we have
carefully updated verb forms and wording that may distract modern readers.

Stock or custom editions of Summerside Press titles may be purchased in
bulk for educational, business, ministry, fundraising, or sales promotional
use. For information, please e-mail specialmarkets@summersidepress.com.

Compiled by Barbara Farmer
Cover design by Koechel Peterson & Associates
Interior design by Jeff Jansen | aestheticsoup.net

*Summerside Press™ is an inspirational publisher offering fresh, irresistible
books to uplift the heart and engage the mind.*

Printed in USA.

Contents

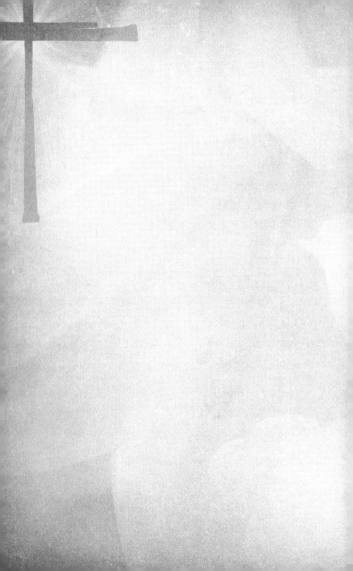

Introduction

*T*he central theme of Easter is the triumphant resurrection of Jesus Christ. That alone is a powerful message. But even more, behind the ministry and the beyond the sacrifice, Jesus is the embodiment of the greatest gift of all: God's amazing love.

Amazing Love is a special collection of quotations and Scriptures set in uplifting and awe-inspiring themes that reflect the love of the Father through the gift of His Son. Woven through this Easter treasury is the life-saving and life-changing story of Jesus' journey to the cross as told by the apostle Luke.

These inspiring words help us to worship the Father for His plan to save us, rejoice in the Son for His willingness to die, and praise the Holy Spirit for opening our hearts to this eternal treasure. May the message of Easter fill you with God's deep love and move you to love others as He first loved us.

Christ never took anything more seriously than the cup of redemption He faced that last Passover supper. His body would soon be broken so that the Bread of life could be distributed to all who would sit at His table. The wine of His blood would be poured into the new wineskins of all who would partake. It was time's perfect night—a night when the last few stitches of a centuries-old Passover thread would be woven onto the canvas of earth in the shape of a cross.

BETH MOORE

The Passover Lamb

Then came the day of Unleavened Bread on which the Passover lamb had to be sacrificed.... When the hour came, Jesus and his apostles reclined at the table.... And he took bread, gave thanks and broke it, and gave it to them, saying, "This is my body given for you; do this in remembrance of me." In the same way, after the supper he took the cup, saying, "This cup is the new covenant in my blood, which is poured out for you."

Luke 22:7, 14, 19–20 niv

His Great Love

*M*ost people would not be willing to die for an upright person, though someone might perhaps be willing to die for a person who is especially good. But God showed his great love for us by sending Christ to die for us while we were still sinners. And since we have been made right in God's sight by the blood of Christ, he will certainly save us from God's condemnation. For since our friendship with God was restored by the death of his Son while we were still his enemies, we will certainly be saved through the life of his Son. So now we can rejoice in our wonderful new relationship with God because our Lord Jesus Christ has made us friends of God.

ROMANS 5:7–11 NLT

Therefore, there is now no condemnation for those who are in Christ Jesus, because through Christ Jesus the law of the Spirit who gives life has set you free from the law of sin and death. For what the law was powerless to do because it was weakened by the flesh, God did by sending his own Son in the likeness of sinful flesh to be a sin offering.

ROMANS 8:1–3 NIV

Love is there for us, love so great that it does not turn its face away from us. That Love is Jesus. We can dare to hope and believe again.

GLORIA GAITHER

The Lord's Supper

The purpose of the Lord's Supper is to receive
from Christ the nourishment and strength and
hope and joy that come from feasting our souls
on all that He purchased for us on the cross,
especially His own fellowship.

JOHN PIPER

Bread of the world, in mercy broken,
Wine of the soul, in mercy shed,
By whom the words of life were spoken,
And in whose death our sins are dead:
Look on the heart by sorrow broken,
Look on the tears by sinners shed;
And be Thy feast to us the token
That by Thy grace our souls are fed.

REGINALD HEBER

*T*he wonder of our Lord is that He is so
accessible to us in the common things of our
lives: the cup of water...breaking of the bread...
welcoming children into our arms...
fellowship over a meal...giving thanks.

<small>NANCIE CARMICHAEL</small>

*T*hen he took a cup, and when he had given
thanks, he gave it to them, saying, "Drink from it,
all of you. This is my blood of the covenant, which
is poured out for many for the forgiveness of sins."

<small>MATTHEW 26:27–28 NIV</small>

*C*hrist is our Passover!
And we will keep the feast
With the new leaven,
The bread of heaven:
All welcome, even the least!

<small>A.R. THOMPSON</small>

The Grace of God

Because of his great love for us, God, who is rich in mercy, made us alive with Christ even when we were dead in transgressions—it is by grace you have been saved. And God raised us up with Christ and seated us with him in the heavenly realms in Christ Jesus, in order that in the coming ages he might show the incomparable riches of his grace, expressed in his kindness to us in Christ Jesus. For it is by grace you have been saved, through faith—and this is not from yourselves, it is the gift of God—not by works, so that no one can boast.

EPHESIANS 2:4–9 NIV

Grace means that God already loves us as much as an infinite God can possibly love.

PHILIP YANCEY

*G*race is something you can never get
but can only be given. There's no way
to earn it or deserve it or bring it about
any more than you can deserve the taste of
raspberries and cream or earn good looks....
A good night's sleep is grace
and so are good dreams.
Most tears are grace. The smell of rain is grace.
Somebody loving you is grace.

FREDERICK BUECHNER

*G*od's grace is the oil that fills
the lamp of love.

HENRY WARD BEECHER

Made Whole

The precious truth of Jesus' power as
Redeemer is that He has a plan and an ability to
progressively restore the broken parts of human
experience and to reproduce a whole person.

JACK HAYFORD

How blessed is God! And what a blessing he is!
He's the Father of our Master, Jesus Christ, and
takes us to the high places of blessing in him.
Long before he laid down earth's foundations,
he had us in mind, had settled on us as the focus
of his love, to be made whole and holy by his love.
Long, long ago he decided to adopt us into his
family through Jesus Christ. (What pleasure
he took in planning this!) He wanted us to enter
into the celebration of his lavish gift-giving
by the hand of his beloved Son.

EPHESIANS 1:3–6 MSG

God did not tell us to follow Him because
He needed our help, but because He knew
that loving Him would make us whole.

IRENAEUS

Lord, let the glow of Your love
Through my whole being shine;
Fill me with gladness from above
And hold me by strength divine.

MARGARET FISHBACK POWERS

May God himself,
the God who makes everything holy and whole,
make you holy and whole.

1 THESSALONIANS 5:23 MSG

Our Divine Imprint

The God of the universe—the One who created everything and holds it all in His hand—created each of us in His image, to bear His likeness, His imprint. It is only when Christ dwells within our hearts, radiating the pure light of His love through our humanity, that we discover who we are and what we were intended to be.

Wendy Moore

In the very beginning it was God who formed us by His Word. He made us in His own image. God was spirit and He gave us a spirit so that He could come into us and mingle His own life with our life.

Madame Jeanne Guyon

*Y*ou are a little less than angels,
crown of creation, image of God.
Each person is a revelation, a transfiguration,
a waiting for Him to manifest Himself.

EDWARD FARRELL

*M*ade in His image, we can have real meaning,
and we can have real knowledge through what
He has communicated to us.

FRANCIS SCHAEFFER

*I*n Him all the fullness of Deity dwells in bodily
form, and in Him you have been made complete.

COLOSSIANS 2:9–10 NASB

*E*very single act of love
bears the imprint of God.

Rare Beauty

*B*lue skies with white clouds on summer days.
A myriad of stars on clear moonlit nights.
Tulips and roses and violets and dandelions
and daisies. Bluebirds and laughter
and sunshine and Easter. See how He loves us!

ALICE CHAPIN

*I*t is an extraordinary and beautiful thing
that God, in creation...works with the beauty
of matter; the reality of things; the discoveries
of the senses, all five of them; so that we,
in turn, may hear the grass growing; see a face
springing to life in love and laughter....
The offerings of creation...our glimpses of truth.

MADELEINE L'ENGLE

*E*aster spells out beauty,
the rare beauty of new life.

S. D. GORDON

14

The beauty of the earth, the beauty of the sky, the order of the stars, the sun, the moon...their very loveliness is their confession of God: for who made these lovely mutable things, but He who is Himself unchangeable beauty?

AUGUSTINE

Nothing can compare to the beauty and greatness of the soul in which our King dwells in His full majesty. No earthly fire can compare with the light of its blazing love. No stronghold can compare with its ability to endure forever.

TERESA OF AVILA

Worship the LORD
in the beauty of holiness!

PSALM 96:9 NKJV

*N*ever minimize the moment by thinking God couldn't have removed the cup.... Do not subtract God's freedom of choice from this picture. God can relent if He chooses. After all, He is the Sovereign of the world. That God could have stopped the process yet didn't is a matchless demonstration of love.... The request Christ placed before the Father ought to make us catch our breath. It ascended to heaven through wails of grief. God's Beloved was overwhelmed with sorrow to the point of death.... Do we think God sat upon His throne unmoved?

BETH MOORE

In the Garden

*A*nd he came out and went, as was his custom, to the Mount of Olives, and the disciples followed him.... And he withdrew from them about a stone's throw, and knelt down and prayed, saying, "Father, if you are willing, remove this cup from me. Nevertheless, not my will, but yours, be done." And there appeared to him an angel from heaven, strengthening him. And being in an agony he prayed more earnestly; and his sweat became like great drops of blood falling down to the ground.

LUKE 22:39, 41–44 ESV

Beautiful Surrender

*J*esus' prayer in the Garden of Gethsemane is amazing, for so many reasons. One is just that it's so impossible. He was God. Creator, Ruler, Sustainer. And yet there He is, with His face pressed to the ground, crying out to the heavens for mercy.

When we view Him through the lens of His humanity, though, it's almost just as amazing. For what human, facing torture and death on a cross, would be able to submit to that fate as the will of God? Only a hero. Only one totally focused on His mission. And only one who truly trusted in the sovereignty and goodness of His God.

GWEN FORD FAULKENBERRY

Letting go of what the world calls safety and surrendering to the Lord is our insurance of fulfillment. Christ knew His Father and offered himself unreservedly into His hands. If we let ourselves be lost for His sake, trusting the same God as Lord of all, we shall find safety where Christ found His, in the bosom of the Father.

ELISABETH ELLIOT

*He fell with His face to the ground
and prayed, "My Father, if it is possible,
may this cup be taken from me.
Yet not as I will, but as you will."*

MATTHEW 26:39 NIV

He Understands

God possesses infinite knowledge
and an awareness which is uniquely His.
At all times, even in the midst of any type
of suffering, I can realize that He knows,
loves, watches, understands,
and more than that, He has a purpose.

BILLY GRAHAM

God takes care of His own. He knows
our needs. He anticipates our crises.
He is moved by our weaknesses. He stands ready
to come to our rescue. And at just the right
moment He steps in and proves Himself
as our faithful heavenly Father.

CHARLES SWINDOLL

What matters supremely is not the fact
that I know God, but the larger fact which
underlies it—the fact that *He knows me*.
I am graven on the palms of His hands.
I am never out of His mind. All my knowledge
of Him depends on His sustained initiative
in knowing me. I know Him because He first
knew me, and continues to know me.

J. I. PACKER

If anyone loves God, he is known by Him.

1 CORINTHIANS 8:3 NASB

Pour out your heart to God your Father.
He understands you better than you do.

Gethsemane

*A*s Jesus stepped into the garden, you were in His prayers. As Jesus looked into heaven, you were in His vision. As Jesus dreamed of the day when we will be where He is, He saw you there. His final prayer was about you. His final pain was for you. His final passion was you.

MAX LUCADO

*I*n the school of Gethsemane...
we have the incarnate Son praying through His tears and not receiving what He asks. Here we have the complete laying down of human will. Here we have the perfect flowing into the will of the Father.

RICHARD J. FOSTER

*H*e [Jesus] carried our sin, our captivity, and our suffering, and He did not carry it in vain. He carried it away.

Karl Barth

*J*esus came with [the disciples] to a place called Gethsemane.... Then He said to them, "My soul is exceedingly sorrowful, even to death. Stay here and watch with Me." He went a little farther and fell on His face, and prayed, saying, "O My Father, if it is possible, let this cup pass from Me; nevertheless, not as I will, but as You *will*."

Matthew 26:36, 38–39 NKJV

*H*e suffered so much solely in order to cry out to us that He loves us.

Charles de Foucauld

Blessed Assurance

So wait before the Lord. Wait in the stillness.
And in that stillness, assurance will come to you.
You will know that you are heard; you will know
that your Lord ponders the voice of your
humble desires; you will hear quiet words
spoken to you yourself, perhaps to your
grateful surprise and refreshment.

AMY CARMICHAEL

Let us draw near to God with a sincere heart
and with the full assurance that faith brings,
having our hearts sprinkled to cleanse us from a
guilty conscience and having our bodies washed
with pure water. Let us hold unswervingly to the
hope we profess, for he who promised is faithful.

HEBREWS 10:22–23 NIV

*I*n those times I can't seem to find God, I rest in
the assurance He knows how to find me.

NEVA COYLE

*P*eace *with* God brings the peace *of* God.
It is a peace that settles our nerves,
fills our mind, floods our spirit, and in the midst
of the uproar around us, gives us the
assurance that everything is all right.

BOB MUMFORD

*B*e assured, if you walk with Him
and look to Him and expect help from Him,
He will never fail you.

GEORGE MUELLER

God Does Care

*J*esus "offered up loud cries and tears to the one who could save him from death." But of course he was not saved from death. Is it too much to say that Jesus himself asked the question that haunts...most of us at one time or another: Does God care?...

Jesus faced pain...much as I do. He experienced sorrow, fear, abandonment, and something approaching even desperation. Yet he endured because he knew that at the center of the universe lived his Father, a God of love he could trust regardless of how things appeared at the time. Jesus' response to suffering people provides a glimpse into the heart of God. God is not the unmoved Absolute, but rather the Loving One who draws near.

PHILIP YANCEY

If you believe in God, it is not too difficult to believe that He is concerned about the universe and all the events on this earth. But the really staggering message of the Bible is that this same God cares deeply about you and your identity and the events of your life.

BRUCE LARSON

God remembered us when we were down,
His love never quits....
Takes care of everyone in time of need.
His love never quits.

PSALM 136:23, 25 MSG

Always There

We need never shout across the spaces to an
absent God. He is nearer than our own soul,
closer than our most secret thoughts.

A. W. TOZER

Late have I loved You, O beauty so ancient
and so new. Late have I loved You!
You were within me while I have gone
outside to seek You. Unlovely myself,
I rushed towards all those lovely things
You had made. And always You were with me.

AUGUSTINE

Always be in a state of expectancy, and see that
you leave room for God to come in as He likes.

OSWALD CHAMBERS

God is always present in the temple of your heart...His home. And when you come in to meet Him there, you find that it is the one place of deep satisfaction where every longing is met.

Tuck [this] thought into your heart today. Treasure it. Your Father God cares about your daily everythings that concern you.

KAY ARTHUR

I know the LORD is always with me.
I will not be shaken, for he is right beside me.
No wonder my heart is glad, and I rejoice.

PSALM 16:8–9 NLT

*W*hat is our response to someone betraying
us? Do we sulk away and complain to others
about the incident? Do we lash out in anger and
let revenge take control? Or do we confront with
truth and love. Jesus looked Judas in the eye, and
even with His heart hurting over the betrayal, He
turned moments later to heal another wounded
man. Oh may we be like Jesus, so sure of God's
love that we can turn hurt into healing.

BARBARA FARMER

Judas Betrays Jesus

While he was still speaking a crowd
came up, and the man who was called Judas,
one of the Twelve, was leading them.
He approached Jesus to kiss him, but Jesus
asked him, "Judas, are you betraying the Son
of Man with a kiss?" When Jesus' followers saw
what was going to happen, they said, "Lord,
should we strike with our swords?"
And one of them struck the servant of
the high priest, cutting off his right ear.
But Jesus answered, "No more of this!"
And he touched the man's ear and healed him.

LUKE 22:47–51 NIV

The Love of God

Who shall separate us from the love of Christ?
Shall trouble or hardship or persecution or
famine or nakedness or danger or sword?... No,
in all these things we are more than conquerors
through him who loved us. For I am convinced
that neither death nor life, neither angels nor
demons, neither the present nor the future,
nor any powers, neither height nor depth,
nor anything else in all creation, will be able
to separate us from the love of God
that is in Christ Jesus our Lord.

ROMANS 8:35, 37–39 NIV

Our love to God arises out of our emptiness;
God's love to us out of His fullness.

HANNAH MORE

*W*e have a Father in heaven who is almighty,
who loves His children as He loves His
only-begotten Son, and whose very joy
and delight it is to [comfort] and help them
at all times and under all circumstances.

GEORGE MUELLER

*N*othing can separate you from His love,
absolutely nothing.... God is enough for time,
and God is enough for eternity. God is enough!

HANNAH WHITALL SMITH

*A*ll the things in this world are gifts
and signs of God's love to us. The whole world
is a love letter from God.

PETER KREEFT

He Is More

Jesus is the Savior, but He is even more than that!
He is more than a Forgiver of our sins.
He is even more than our Provider of eternal life.
He is our Redeemer! He is the One who is ready
to recover and restore what the power of sin
and death has taken from us.

JACK HAYFORD

In that place of humble thanks, God exalts
and gives more gifts and more of Himself.
Which humbles and lays the soul down lower.
And [our] good God responds with greater gifts
of grace and even more of Himself.

ANN VOSKAMP

Wonderful the matchless grace of Jesus,
Deeper than the mighty rolling sea;
Wonderful grace, all sufficient for me, for even me.
Broader than the scope of my transgressions,
Greater far than all my sin and shame,
O magnify the precious Name of Jesus.
Praise His Name!

HALDOR LILLENAS

GOD is higher than anything and anyone,
outshining everything you can see in the skies.
Who can compare with GOD, our God,
so majestically enthroned.

PSALM 115:4 MSG

You're Invited

*A*re you tired? Worn out? Burned out on
religion? Come to me. Get away with me
and you'll recover your life. I'll show you how
to take a real rest. Walk with me and work
with me—watch how I do it. Learn the unforced
rhythms of grace. I won't lay anything heavy
or ill-fitting on you. Keep company with me
and you'll learn to live freely and lightly.

MATTHEW 11:28–30 MSG

[*G*od] is looking for people who will come in
simple dependence upon His grace,
and rest in simple faith upon His greatness.
At this very moment, He's looking at you.

JACK HAYFORD

*I*t's like an invitation to visit with God,
to watch the clouds break up and disappear,
leaving behind a blue patch of sky and bright
sunshine that is so warm upon my face.
It's a glimpse of divinity; a kiss from heaven.

*Y*ou've always given me breathing room,
a place to get away from it all,
a lifetime pass to your safe-house,
an open invitation as your guest.

PSALM 61:3 MSG

---

*G*od waits for us in the inner sanctuary
of the soul. He welcomes us there.

RICHARD J. FOSTER

His Purpose

So the main question is not, Which humans brought about the death of Jesus but, What did the death of Jesus bring about for humans—including Jews and Muslims and Buddhists and Hindus and nonreligious secularists—and all people everywhere? When it is all said and done, the most crucial question is: Why? Why did Christ suffer and die? Not why in the sense of *cause*, but why in the sense of *purpose*?

JOHN PIPER

I did not come to abolish the law of Moses or the writings of the prophets. No, I came to accomplish their purpose. I tell you the truth, until heaven and earth disappear, not even the smallest detail of God's law will disappear until its purpose is achieved.

MATTHEW 5:17–18 NLT

Death was not Jesus' penalty; it was His destiny.
It was not His lot in life; it was His mission.
It was not His unavoidable fate; it was His
purpose statement for coming to earth
that first Christmas: "Born to die."

BILL CROWDER

Because Christ fulfilled His purpose
through His death and resurrection,
I have hope, my life has meaning, and others
will know Him for I can't keep silent.

BARBARA FARMER

The plans of the LORD stand firm forever,
the purposes of his heart through all generations.

PSALM 33:11 NIV

A Safe Journey

Do not be afraid of the terrors of the night,
nor the arrow that flies in the day.
Do not dread the disease that stalks in darkness,
nor the disaster that strikes at midday....
If you make the LORD your refuge,
if you make the Most High your shelter,
no evil will conquer you....
For he will order his angels
to protect you wherever you go.
They will hold you up with their hands
so you won't even hurt your foot on a stone....
The LORD says, "I will rescue those who love me.
I will protect those who trust in my name."

PSALM 91:5–6, 9–12, 14 NLT

God loves to look at us, and loves it when we
will look back at Him. Even when we try to run
away from our troubles...God will find us,
bless us, even when we feel most alone, unsure....
God will find a way to let us know that
He is with us *in this place*, wherever we are.

KATHLEEN NORRIS

It is God to whom and with whom we travel,
and while He is the End of our journey,
He is also at every stopping place.

ELISABETH ELLIOT

*There is no safer place to be
than in the Father's hands.*

Here and Now

The great Easter truth is not that we are to live newly after death, but that we are to be new here and now by the power of the resurrection.

PHILLIPS BROOKS

We died and were buried with Christ by baptism. And just as Christ was raised from the dead by the glorious power of the Father, now we also may live new lives.

ROMANS 6:4 NLT

Isn't this the crux of the gospel? The good news that all those living in the land of the shadow of death have been birthed into new life, new light, that the transfiguration of a suffering world has begun, and behold, He is making all things new.

ANN VOSKAMP

The resurrection that awaits us beyond
physical death will be but the glorious
consummation of the risen life
which already we have in Christ.

D. T. NILES

Through faith in His death and resurrection,
we can be forgiven of our sin, be reconciled
to the Father, and come back into the purpose
for which we were originally created.

ANNE GRAHAM LOTZ

To be with God, in whatever stage of being,
under whatever conditions of existence,
is to be in heaven.

DORA GREENWELL

*That God can bring good out of our mistakes
is part of the wonder of His gracious sovereignty.
The Jesus who restored Peter after his denial and
corrected his course more than once after that is our
Savior today and He has not changed.*

J. I. PACKER

Peter Denies Jesus

So they arrested him and led him to the high priest's home. And Peter followed at a distance. The guards lit a fire in the middle of the courtyard and sat around it, and Peter joined them there. A servant girl noticed him in the firelight and began staring at him. Finally she said, "This man was one of Jesus' followers!" But Peter denied it.... After a while someone else looked at him and said, "You must be one of them!" "No, man, I'm not!" Peter retorted. About an hour later someone else insisted, "This must be one of them, because he is a Galilean, too." But Peter said, "Man, I don't know what you are talking about." And immediately, while he was still speaking, the rooster crowed. At that moment the Lord turned and looked at Peter.

LUKE 22:54–61 NLT

He Cannot Forget Us

There was a time when if [Jesus] could have, He would have turned His back on the whole mess and gone away. But He couldn't. He couldn't because He saw you. He saw you betrayed by those you love. He saw you with a body which gets sick and a heart which grows weak. He saw you in your own garden of gnarled trees and sleeping friends. He saw you staring into the pit of your own failures and the mouth of your own grave. He saw you in your own garden of Gethsemane and he didn't want you to be alone.... He would rather go to hell for you than to heaven without you.

MAX LUCADO

The great thing to remember is that, though our feelings come and go, His love for us does not.

C. S. LEWIS

[*Jesus*] played life against death and death against life...so that by His death He destroyed our death, and to give us life He spent His own bodily life. With love, then, He has so drawn us and with His kindness so conquered our malice that every heart should be won over.

CATHERINE OF SIENNA

I will not forget you! See, I have engraved you on the palms of my hands.

ISAIAH 49:15–16 NIV

Full Restoration

*W*hatever your loss, pain, failure,
or brokenness, Jesus Christ is fully capable of
bringing about change unto full restoration.
Just as His resurrection power brings new life,
His redemption power brings new hope.
He is able, for He's more than a Savior!
He's your Redeemer who promises that
He will give "beauty for ashes,
the oil of joy for mourning" (Isaiah 61:3).

JACK HAYFORD

*W*hatever mistakes we may make, we shall
come safely home. Slippings and strayings there
will be, no doubt, but the everlasting arms are
beneath us; we shall be caught, rescued, restored.
This is God's promise; this is how good He is.

J. I. PACKER

*C*reate in me a pure heart, O God,
and renew a steadfast spirit within me.
Do not cast me from your presence
or take your Holy Spirit from me.
Restore to me the joy of your salvation
and grant me a willing spirit, to sustain me.

PSALM 51:10–12 NIV

*B*e still, and in the quiet moments,
listen to the voice of your heavenly Father.
His words can renew your spirit...no one knows
you and your needs like He does.

JANET L. SMITH

All Is Well

*I*t's usually through our hard times, the
unexpected and not-according-to-plan times,
that we experience God in more intimate ways.
We discover an unquenchable longing to know
Him more. It's a passion that isn't concerned
that life fall within certain predictable lines,
but a passion that pursues God and knows He is
relentless in His pursuit of each one of us.

WENDY MOORE

A living, loving God can and does make
His presence felt, can and does speak to us
in the silence of our hearts, can and does
warm and caress us till we no longer doubt
that He is near, that He is here.

BRENNAN MANNING

If one is joyful, it means that one is faithfully
living for God, and that nothing else counts; and
if one gives joy to others, one is doing God's work.
With joy without and joy within, all is well.

JANET ERSKINE STUART

*L*ord, you have been our dwelling place
throughout all generations.
Before the mountains were born
or you brought forth the earth and the world,
from everlasting to everlasting you are God.

PSALM 90:1–2 NIV

Before me, even as behind,
God is, and all is well.

JOHN GREENLEAF WHITTIER

New Life

*S*ince we believe that Christ died for all, we also believe that we have all died to our old life. He died for everyone so that those who receive his new life will no longer live for themselves. Instead, they will live for Christ, who died and was raised for them. So we have stopped evaluating others from a human point of view. At one time we thought of Christ merely from a human point of view. How differently we know him now! This means that anyone who belongs to Christ has become a new person. The old life is gone; a new life has begun! And all of this is a gift from God.

2 Corinthians 5:14–18 nlt

God's love is like a river springing up
in the Divine Substance and flowing endlessly
through His creation, filling all things with life
and goodness and strength.

THOMAS MERTON

Once more to new creation Awake,
and death gainsay,
For death is swallowed up of life,
And Christ is risen today!

GEORGE NEWELL LOVEJOY

*The resurrection gives my life meaning
and direction and the opportunity to start
over no matter what my circumstances.*

ROBERT FLATT

Rest in Him

My soul finds rest in God alone;
my salvation comes from him.
He alone is my rock and my salvation;
he is my fortress, I will never be shaken....
My salvation and my honor depend on God;
he is my mighty rock, my refuge.
Trust in him at all times, O people;
pour out your hearts to him,
for God is our refuge....
One thing God has spoken,
two things have I heard:
that you, O God, are strong,
and that you, O Lord, are loving.

PSALM 62:1–2, 7–8, 11–12 NIV†

*O*nly Christ himself, who slept in the boat in the storm and then spoke calm to the wind and waves, can stand beside us when we are in a panic and say to us Peace. It will not be explainable. It transcends human understanding. And there is nothing else like it in the whole wide world.

ELISABETH ELLIOT

*R*est in the LORD, and wait patiently for Him.

PSALM 37:7 NKJV

*W*hen God finds a soul that rests in Him and is not easily moved...to this same soul He gives the joy of His presence.

CATHERINE OF GENOA

Our Destiny

This is our destiny in heaven—to be like Christ:
not Christ limited, as He was on earth, to the
confines of time and flesh, but Christ risen, the
great, free, timeless Christ of the Easter morning.

DAVID WINTER

Our confidence in the future is based firmly on
the fact of what God has done for us in Christ.
No matter what our situation may be,
we need never despair because Christ is alive.

BILLY GRAHAM

Recognizing who we are in Christ and aligning
our life with God's purpose for us gives a sense of
destiny.... It gives form and direction to our life.

JEAN FLEMING

I still belong to you;
you hold my right hand.
You guide me with your counsel,
leading me to a glorious destiny.
Whom have I in heaven but you?
I desire you more than anything on earth.
My health may fail, and my spirit may grow weak,
but God remains the strength of my heart;
he is mine forever.

PSALM 73:23–26 NLT

*It is through man's encounter with God
that he reaches his highest destiny.*

CAROL GISH

*Whether we believe it or not,
Jesus is the King of kings, the radiance of God's glory,
the Son of Man. He is the Lord of the spaceless,
fabulous, infinite universe; omniscient, omnipotent,
omnipresent, unspeakably holy, dwelling in
light, unapproachable, changeless...and yet He
condescended to be enclosed in human flesh.*

The Mock Trial

$\mathcal{N}$ow the men who were holding Jesus in custody were mocking him as they beat him. They also blindfolded him and kept asking him, "Prophesy! Who is it that struck you?" And they said many other things against him, blaspheming him.

When day came, the assembly of the elders of the people gathered together, both chief priests and scribes. And they led him away to their council, and they said, "If you are the Christ, tell us." But he said to them, "If I tell you, you will not believe, and if I ask you, you will not answer. But from now on the Son of Man shall be seated at the right hand of the power of God." So they all said, "Are you the Son of God, then?" And he said to them, "You say that I am." Then they said, "What further testimony do we need? We have heard it ourselves from his own lips."

LUKE 22:63–71 ESV

He Walks with Us

In the ultimate alchemy of all history, God took
the worst thing that could possibly happen—the
appalling execution of the innocent Son—and
turned it into the final victory over evil and death.
It was an act of unprecedented cunning, turning
the design of evil into the service of good, an act
that holds within it a promise for all of us.

PHILIP YANCEY

The Lord our shepherd is with us,
in the valley or even in the face of death,
sharing a meal of friendship, giving us
all that we need and more.

MICHAEL NEALE

*T*he LORD is my shepherd;
I shall not want.
He makes me to lie down in green pastures;
He leads me beside the still waters.
He restores my soul;
He leads me in the paths of righteousness
For His name's sake.
Yea, though I walk through the valley
of the shadow of death, I will fear no evil;
For You are with me;
Your rod and Your staff, they comfort me.
You prepare a table before me
in the presence of my enemies;
You anoint my head with oil;
My cup runs over.
Surely goodness and mercy shall follow me
All the days of my life;
And I will dwell in the house of the LORD
Forever.

PSALM 23:1–6 NKJV

As Seen in Nature

The deep woods reveal God's presence.
The way the golden sunlight streaks through
the lush greens and browns of a summer wood
is nothing short of divine. In the fall the
profusion of colors makes every leaf a prayer.
Winter's snow transforms the woods into a
cathedral. Even the dark, drab hues of the woods
in early spring speak of hope and resurrection.

RAYMOND K. PETRUCCI

From the world we see, hear, and touch,
we behold inspired visions that reveal God's glory.
In the sun's light, we catch warm rays of grace
and glimpse His eternal design. In the birds' song,
we hear His voice and it reawakens our need
of Him. At the wind's touch, we feel His Spirit
and sense our eternal existence.

WENDY MOORE

I love to think of nature as an unlimited
broadcasting station through which God speaks
to us every hour, if only we will tune in.

GEORGE WASHINGTON CARVER

*B*eauty puts a face on God. When we gaze
at nature, at a loved one, at a work of art,
our soul immediately recognizes
and is drawn to the face of God.

MARGARET BROWNLEY

*T*he heavens declare the glory of God;
And the firmament shows His handiwork.

PSALM 19:1 NKJV

The more I study nature,
the more I am amazed at the Creator.

LOUIS PASTEUR

He Pays Attention

God gets down on His knees among us;
gets on our level and shares Himself with us.
He does not reside afar off and send diplomatic
messages, He kneels among us.... God shares
Himself generously and graciously.

EUGENE PETERSON

If you believe in God, it is not too difficult
to believe that He is concerned about
the universe and all the events on this earth.
But the really staggering message of the Bible
is that this same God cares deeply about you
and your identity and the events of your life.

BRUCE LARSON

I'm not saying that I have this all together, that I have it made. But I am well on my way, reaching out for Christ, who has so wondrously reached out for me.

PHILIPPIANS 3:12 MSG

*T*he God who created, names, and numbers the stars in the heavens also numbers the hairs of my head.... He pays attention to very big things and to very small ones. What matters to me matters to Him, and that changes my life.

ELISABETH ELLIOT

Your unfailing love is as high as the heavens. Your faithfulness reaches to the clouds.

PSALM 57:10 NLT

A Message for Us

What we need to know, of course, is not just that God exists, not just that beyond the steely brightness of the stars there is a cosmic intelligence...but that there is a God right here in the thick of our day-by-day lives who may not be writing messages about Himself in the stars but in one way or another is trying to get messages through our blindness.

FREDERICK BUECHNER

The Empty Tomb had a message for the disciples as it has for us. It says to science and philosophy, "Explain this event." It says to history, "Repeat this event." It says to time, "Blot out this event." It says to faith, "Believe this event."

This resurrection life you received from God is
not a timid, grave-tending life. It's adventurously
expectant, greeting God with a childlike "What's
next, Papa?" God's Spirit touches our spirits and
confirms who we really are. We know who he is,
and we know who we are: Father and children.
And we know we are going to get what's coming
to us—an unbelievable inheritance!

ROMANS 8:15–16 MSG

*Love. No greater theme can be emphasized.
No stronger message can be proclaimed.*

CHARLES SWINDOLL

Redeemed

*D*on't be afraid, I've redeemed you. I've called your name. You're mine. When you're in over your head, I'll be there with you. When you're in rough waters, you will not go down. When you're between a rock and a hard place, it won't be a dead end—Because I am God, your personal God, The Holy of Israel, your Savior. I paid a huge price for you...! *That's* how much you mean to me! *That's* how much I love you!

ISAIAH 43:1–4 MSG

*W*hen we focus on God, the scene changes. He's in control of our lives; nothing lies outside the realm of His redemptive grace. Even when we make mistakes, fail in relationships, or deliberately make bad choices, God can redeem us.

PENELOPE J. STOKES

Your grace, how it's sufficient for me,
    how it carries all my burdens
    and displaces my iniquity.
When the Father gazes down
    no longer does he see
the reflection of a wicked man,
    but the man who died on Calvary.

*It was not with perishable things
such as silver or gold that you were redeemed
    from the empty way of life...
but with the precious blood of Christ.*

1 PETER 1:18–19 NIV

Our Gracious God

The grace of God means something like:
Here is your life. You might never have been,
but you *are* because the party wouldn't have
been complete without you. Here is the world.
Beautiful and terrible things will happen. Don't be
afraid. I am with you. Nothing can ever separate
us. It's for you I created the universe. I love you.

FREDERICK BUECHNER

The LORD longs to be gracious to you;
therefore he will rise up to show you compassion.

ISAIAH 30:18 NIV

His overflowing love delights to make us
partakers of the bounties He graciously imparts.

HANNAH MORE

*G*od makes everything come out right;
  he puts victims back on their feet....
He doesn't endlessly nag and scold,
  nor hold grudges forever.
He doesn't treat us as our sins deserve,
  nor pay us back in full for our wrongs.
As high as heaven is over the earth,
  so strong is his love to those who fear him.
And as far as sunrise is from sunset,
  he has separated us from our sins.

PSALM 103:6, 9–12 MSG

*L*ord...give me only Your love
and Your grace. With this I am rich enough,
and I have no more to ask.

IGNATIUS OF LOYOLA

71

Jesus not only came bearing revolutionary truth about Himself, He bore revolutionary truth about the love of God—and as He bore it, He demonstrated it in His own person, before, during, and after His crucifixion.

EUGENIA PRICE

The Verdict

Then the entire council took Jesus to Pilate, the Roman governor. They began to state their case.... So Pilate asked him, "Are you the king of the Jews?" Jesus replied, "You have said it." Pilate turned to the leading priests and to the crowd and said, "I find nothing wrong with this man!"... Pilate sent him to Herod Antipas.... Herod was delighted at the opportunity to see Jesus, because he had heard about him and had been hoping for a long time to see him perform a miracle.... Then Herod and his soldiers began mocking and ridiculing Jesus. Finally, they put a royal robe on him and sent him back to Pilate.... Pilate argued with them, because he wanted to release Jesus. But they kept shouting, "Crucify him! Crucify him!"... So Pilate sentenced Jesus to die as they demanded.

LUKE 23:1–4, 7–8, 11, 20–21, 24 NLT

Fulfillment

God led Jesus to a cross, not a crown, and yet
that cross ultimately proved to be the gateway to
freedom and forgiveness for every sinner in the
world. God also asks us as Jesus' followers to carry
a cross. Paradoxically, in carrying that cross,
we find liberty and joy and fulfillment.

BILL HYBELS

As redemption creates the life of God in us,
it also creates the things which belong to that life.
The only thing that can possibly satisfy the need
is what created the need. This is the meaning
of redemption—it creates and it satisfies.

OSWALD CHAMBERS

Our fulfillment comes in knowing God's glory,
loving Him for it, and delighting in it.

*T*he "air" which our souls need also envelops all
of us at all times and on all sides.
God is round about us in Christ on every hand,
with many-sided and all-sufficient grace.
All we need to do is to open our hearts.

OLE HALLESBY

*S*atisfy us in the morning with your unfailing love,
that we may sing for joy and be glad all our days.

PSALM 90:14 NIV

We are made for God,
and nothing less will really satisfy us.

BRENNAN MANNING

Indescribable Gift

The highest act of love is the giving of the best
gift, and, if necessary, at the greatest cost,
to the least deserving. That's what God did.
At the loss of His Son's life to the totally
undeserving, God gave the best gift—the display
of the glory of Christ who is the image of God.

JOHN PIPER

God be thanked for that good and perfect gift,
the gift unspeakable: His life, His love,
His very self in Christ Jesus.

MALTBIE D. BABCOCK

Like any other gift, the gift of grace can be
yours only if you'll reach out and take it. Maybe
being able to reach out and take it is a gift too.

FREDERICK BUECHNER

*G*race is the dynamic outpouring of God's loving nature that flows into and through creation in an endless self-offering of healing, love, illumination, and reconciliation. It is a gift that we are free to ignore, reject, ask for, or simply accept.

DR. GERALD G. MAY

*T*hank You, Jesus, for Your unlimited grace that saves me from my sins. I receive Your gift of grace. Transform my life so that I may bring glory and honor to You alone.

MARILYN JANSEN

Thanks be to God for His indescribable gift!

2 CORINTHIANS 9:15 NKJV

Heart of the Matter

The heart...is the human spirit,
and the only thing in us that God
will accept as the basis of our
relationship to Him. It is the
spiritual plane of our natural existence,
the place of truth before God,
from where alone our whole
lives can become eternal.

DALLAS WILLARD

By Jesus' gracious, kindly Spirit,
He moves in our lives, sharing His very own life
with us.... He introduces the exotic fruits of His
own person into the prepared soil of our hearts;
there they take root and flourish.

W. PHILIP KELLER

*W*e invite the Lord to search our hearts to the depths.... This is a scrutiny of love. We boldly speak the words of the Psalmist, "Search me, O God, and know my heart; test me and know my thoughts."

RICHARD J. FOSTER

*O*nce the seeking heart finds God in personal experience there will be no problem about loving Him. To know Him is to love Him and to know Him better is to love Him more.

A. W. TOZER

*H*e who searches our hearts knows the mind of the Spirit, because the Spirit intercedes for God's people in accordance with the will of God.

ROMANS 8:27 NIV

Bring Us Near

What a mind-boggling truth it is that Jesus wants us near—wanted us even when we didn't want Him. He wanted us badly enough to die so that He could bring us near!...
It's hard to comprehend such a radical love. After all, why would He want to be near *me*?...

And yet, when He was on the way to the cross, we were on His mind. He prayed for me—and you— to have His fullness. Not just a little bit of Him. All of the fullness of His joy. We don't have to cringe or coax Him to be near us. He died so that's where He could always stay—near me.

GWEN FORD FAULKENBERRY

I say these things...so that they may have the full measure of my joy within them.

JOHN 17:13 NIV

*G*od is as near as a whispered prayer
No matter the time or place,
Whether skies are blue
And all's right with you,
Or clouds dim the road you face.
In His mercy and great compassion
He will ease, He will help, He will share!
Whatever your lot,
Take heart in the thought:
God's as near as a whispered prayer!

JOHN GILBERT

*G*od still draws near to us in the ordinary,
commonplace, everyday experiences and
places.... He comes in surprising ways.

HENRY GARIEPY

You Can Count on Him

*I*t is on the unshakable fact of the resurrection
of Christ from the dead that I base my faith
in God's utter integrity and faithfulness.
He let Jesus die—but only because He would
raise Him again. You can count on Him!
You can stake your faith on God—the God
of Jesus Christ. He will keep His word.

Leighton Ford

*B*ecause God is responsible for our welfare,
we are told to cast all our care upon Him,
for He cares for us. God says, "I'll take the
burden—don't give it a thought—leave it to Me."
God is keenly aware that we are dependent upon
Him for life's necessities.

Billy Graham

*B*e content with who you are....
God's strong hand is on you; he'll promote you
at the right time. Live carefree before God;
he is most careful with you.

1 PETER 5:7 MSG

*W*e may...depend upon God's promises, for...
He will be as good as His word. He is so kind that
He cannot deceive us, so true that He cannot
break His promise.

MATTHEW HENRY

*T*he more we depend on God
the more dependable we find He is.

SIR CLIFF RICHARD

His Eternal Love

*G*od, who is love—who is, if I may say it this
way, made out of love—simply cannot help but
shed blessing on blessing upon us. We do not
need to beg, for He simply cannot help it!

HANNAH WHITALL SMITH

*T*he LORD is like a father to his children,
tender and compassionate to those who fear him.
For he knows how weak we are;
he remembers we are only dust.
Our days on earth are like grass;
like wildflowers, we bloom and die.
The wind blows, and we are gone—
as though we had never been here.
But the love of the LORD remains forever....
The LORD has made the heavens his throne;
from there he rules over everything.

PSALM 103:13–17, 19 NLT

The kiss of eternal life, and the warm embrace of God's Word, are so sweet, and bring such pleasure, that you can never become bored with them; you always want more.

HILDEGARD OF BINGEN

The reason we can dare to risk loving others is that "God has for Christ's sake loved us." Think of it! We are loved eternally, totally, individually, unreservedly! Nothing can take God's love away.

GLORIA GAITHER

Love has its source in God,
for love is the very essence of His being.

KAY ARTHUR

As the last spoonfuls of sand slipped through
the hourglass, surely the blood pumped harder
through His veins, overworking His heart.
Would God have allowed Him to forego
the tightness of dreadful anticipation in His chest?
Would He have interfered with His Son experiencing
the full gamut of the human body's involuntary
anticipation? Did God allow His Son's hands to
shake? Oh yes, I think Christ felt every bit of it.

BETH MOORE

On the Cross

Two other men, both criminals, were also led out with him to be executed. When they came to the place called the Skull, they crucified him there, along with the criminals—one on his right, the other on his left. Jesus said, "Father, forgive them, for they do not know what they are doing."... There was a written notice above him, which read: THIS IS THE KING OF THE JEWS. One of the criminals who hung there hurled insults at him: "Aren't you the Messiah? Save yourself and us!" But the other criminal rebuked him.... "We are getting what our deeds deserve. But this man has done nothing wrong." Then he said, "Jesus, remember me when you come into your kingdom." Jesus answered him, "Truly I tell you, today you will be with me in paradise."

LUKE 23:32–34, 38–43 NIV

Arms Opened Wide

Never were God's arms opened so wide
as they were on the Roman cross. One arm
extending back into history and the other
reaching into the future. An embrace of
forgiveness offered for anyone who'll come.
A hen gathering her chicks. A father receiving
his own. A redeemer redeeming the world.
No wonder they call Him the Savior.

MAX LUCADO

When we love someone, we want to be with
them, and we view their love for us with great
honor even if they are not a person of great rank.
For this reason—and not because of our great
rank—God values our love. So much, in fact,
that He suffered greatly on our behalf.

JOHN CHRYSOSTOM

He did not retaliate when he was insulted,
nor threaten revenge when he suffered.
He left his case in the hands of God,
who always judges fairly. He personally carried
our sins in his body on the cross so that we can
be dead to sin and live for what is right.
By his wounds you are healed.

1 PETER 2:23–24 NLT

We are of such value to God that He came
to live among us...and to guide us home.
He will go to any length to seek us,
even to being lifted high upon the cross
to draw us back to Himself.

CATHERINE OF SIENNA

You Are Valuable

Our greatness rests solely on the fact
that God in His incomprehensible goodness
has bestowed His love upon us. God does not
love us because we are so valuable;
we are valuable because God loves us.

HELMUT THIELICKE

Look at the lilies and how they grow.
They don't work or make their clothing,
yet Solomon in all his glory was not
dressed as beautifully as they are.
And if God cares so wonderfully for flowers...
he will certainly care for you.

LUKE 12:27–28 NLT

The devil has convinced so many people that they are worthless. Each of us needs to stop and remember the cross—at the cross we will discover our true value—for it is here that we discover the price God was willing to pay for us, the depth of His love, and how much we are worth to Him.

Roy Lessin

The value of a person is not measured on an applause meter; it is measured in the heart and mind of God. Any believer can rest assured, for on God's scale, the needle always reads high.

John Fisher

We do not have to act or look certain ways to be loved and undergirded and accepted. We are valued because of Jesus' work of redemption on the cross.

Gloria Gaither

God Wants You

It may seem strange to think that God wants
to spend time with us, but...think about it.
If God went to all the trouble to come to earth,
to live the life that He did, to die for us,
then there's got to be a hunger and a passion
behind that. We think of prayer as an
"ought to," but in reality it is a response to
God's passionate love for us. We need to
refocus on the fact that God is waiting
for us to show up and be with Him
and that our presence truly touches Him.

Dr. Henry Cloud

*G*od wants you to know Him
as personally as He knows you.
He craves a genuine relationship with you.

Tom Richards

The Lord's chief desire is to reveal
Himself to you.... He touches you,
and His touch is so delightful that,
more than ever, you are drawn inwardly to Him.

MADAME JEANNE GUYON

When God, our kind and loving Savior God,
stepped in, he saved us.... Our Savior Jesus
poured out new life so generously. God's gift has
restored our relationship with him and given
us back our lives. And there's more life to come—
an eternity of life! You can count on this.

TITUS 3:4–8 MSG

*God loves you! He wants you to know Him,
and He is sufficient for your every need.*

ANNE GRAHAM LOTZ

Good Friday

Good Friday is the mirror held up by Jesus so that we can see ourselves in all our stark reality, and then it turns us to that cross and to His eyes and we hear these words, "Father, forgive them, for they know not what they do." That's us! And so we know beyond a shadow of a doubt that if we say we have no sin, we deceive ourselves. We see in that cross a love so amazing, so divine, that it loves us even when we turn away from it, or spurn it, or crucify it. There is no faith in Jesus without understanding that on the cross we see into the heart of God and find it filled with mercy for the sinner, whoever he or she may be.

ROBERT G. TRACHE

When I survey the wondrous cross
On which the Prince of Glory died,
My richest gain I count but loss,
And pour contempt on all my pride....
See from His head, His hands, His feet,
Sorrow and love flow mingled down,
Did e'er such love and sorrow meet,
Or thorns compose so rich a crown?...
Were the whole realm of nature mine,
That were an offering far too small;
Love so amazing, so divine,
Demands my soul, my life, my all.

Isaac Watts

The strongest evidence of love is sacrifice.

Caroline Fry

Divine Romance

We are so preciously loved by God that we
cannot even comprehend it. No created being
can ever know how much and how sweetly and
tenderly God loves them. It is only with the help
of His grace that we are able to persevere in
spiritual contemplation with endless wonder at
His high, surpassing, immeasurable love which
our Lord in His goodness has for us.

JULIAN OF NORWICH

To fall in love with God is the greatest
of all romances, to seek Him
the greatest of all adventures, to find Him
the greatest human achievement.

AUGUSTINE

Look deep within yourself and recognize what brings life and grace into your heart. It is this that can be shared with those around you. You are loved by God. This is an inspiration to love.

CHRISTOPHER DE VINCK

The miracle of Easter came to me personally.... He loves me. He loves me. It's like the riddle people say while picking petals from a flower, except that there's no He loves me not. No possibility of that, because of Calvary, because of the cross.

GWEN FORD FAULKENBERRY

God is sheer beauty, all-generous in love, loyal always and ever.

PSALM 100:5 MSG

*God the Son takes the body and human soul
of Jesus, and, through that, the whole environment
of Nature, all the creaturely predicament,
into His own being.... The pure light walks the earth;
the darkness, received into the heart of Deity,
is there swallowed up. Where, except in uncreated
light, can the darkness be drowned?*

C. S. LEWIS

The Death of Jesus

By this time it was noon, and darkness fell
across the whole land until three o'clock.
The light from the sun was gone. And suddenly,
the curtain in the sanctuary of the Temple was
torn down the middle. Then Jesus shouted,
"Father, I entrust my spirit into your hands!"
And with those words he breathed his last.
When the Roman officer overseeing the execution
saw what had happened, he worshiped God
and said, "Surely this man was innocent."
And when all the crowd that came to see the
crucifixion saw what had happened, they went
home in deep sorrow. But Jesus' friends,
including the women who had followed him
from Galilee, stood at a distance watching.

LUKE 23:44–49 NLT

The Nails

*In the cellar of your heart lurk the ghosts
of yesterday's sins. Sins you've confessed;
errors of which you've repented; damage you've
done your best to repair.... Do yourself a favor.
Purge your cellar. Exorcise your basement.
Take the Roman nails of Calvary and board
up the door. And remember...He forgot.*

MAX LUCADO

*You were dead because of your sins and
because your sinful nature was not yet cut away.
Then God made you alive with Christ,
for he forgave all our sins. He canceled
the record of the charges against us
and took it away by nailing it to the cross.*

COLOSSIANS 2:13–14 NLT

At the cross Christ triumphed over
the cosmic powers—defeating them not with
power but with self-giving love. The cross of
Christ may have assured the final outcome,
but battles remain for us to fight.... In all these
sufferings, large and small, there is the assurance
of a deeper level of meaning, of a sharing
in Christ's own redemptive victory.

PHILIP YANCEY

Jesus cannot forget us;
we have been graven
on the palms of His hands.

LOIS PICILLO

His All For You

When Jesus died on the cross, He was giving
"all He had" to pay the price for all the wrong
things you've ever done. In your heart,
for just a moment, would you walk up that hill the
Bible calls Skull Hill and stand quietly at the foot
of that cross where the Son of God is pouring
out His life for you. Look at Him dying for you!
You are not worthless! But you'll never know
how valuable you are until you give yourself
to the One who died to buy you back.

RON HUTCHCRAFT

God proved His love on the cross.
When Christ hung, and bled, and died,
it was God saying to the world, "I love you."

BILLY GRAHAM

On that terrible, wonderful day,
God's goodness and kindness were directed
toward you. God forsook His own Son...
so that He would never have to forsake you!
And because of those dark hours
two thousand years ago, God can say to [you],
"I will never leave you...I will never forsake you."

JONI EARECKSON TADA

The LORD himself goes before you
and will be with you; he will never leave you
nor forsake you.

DEUTERONOMY 31:8 NIV

Covenant of Love

Christianity is founded on a promise. Faith involves waiting on a promise. Our hope is based on a promise. God promised He would be "with us," not as an unseen ethereal force, but in the form of a person with a name: Jesus.

MICHAEL CARD

If the Lord be with us, we have no cause of fear. His eye is upon us, His arm over us, His ear open to our prayer—His grace sufficient, His promise unchangeable.

JOHN NEWTON

At the cross, God swore by Himself that He's committed to you. There is nothing you will ever do, nothing you will ever fail to do, nothing you could ever do, nothing you could ever fail to do.... There is nothing that can or will ever, *ever*, *EVER* break the covenant. You didn't do anything to earn it, and you can't do anything to lose it. All you have to do is receive it by trusting everything completely to Him.

ANNE GRAHAM LOTZ

He who did not spare his own Son, but gave him up for us all—how will he not also, along with him, graciously give us all things?

ROMANS 8:32 NIV

The Only Way

That fullest life itself dawns from nothing
but Calvary darkness and tomb-cave black
into the radiance of Easter morning.
Out of the darkness of the Cross,
the world transfigures into New Life.
There is no other way.

ANN VOSKAMP

The way of Love is the way of the cross,
and it is only through the cross
that we come to the resurrection.

MALCOLM MUGGERIDGE

Jesus said..."I am the way,
and the truth, and the life;
no one comes to the Father but through Me."

JOHN 14:6 NASB

*I*n Gethsemane [Jesus] really did want the cup to pass, and He asked that it would pass. "If you are willing" was His questioning, His wondering. "Is there any other way? Can people be redeemed by some different means?" The answer—no!

RICHARD J. FOSTER

*W*ithout the Way, there is no going;
Without the Truth, there is no knowing;
Without the Life, there is no living.

THOMAS À KEMPIS

*N*othing is so central to the good news of abundant life in Jesus Christ as the resurrection.

GLORIA GAITHER

Extravagant Love

*B*efore anything else, above all else,
beyond everything else, God loves us.
God loves us extravagantly, ridiculously,
without limit or condition.
God is in love with us...God yearns for us.

ROBERTA BONDI

*O*bserve how Christ loved us. His love was not
cautious but extravagant. He didn't love
in order to get something from us but to give
everything of himself to us. Love like that.

EPHESIANS 5:2 MSG

*G*od will always and forever love us
unconditionally. What He wants from us
is that we love Him back with all our heart.

In extravagance of soul we seek His face.
In generosity of heart, we glean His gentle touch.
In excessiveness of spirit, we love Him and His
love comes back to us a hundredfold.

TRACIA MCCARY RHODES

Nothing we can do will make the Father love us
less; nothing we do can make Him love us more.
He loves us unconditionally with an everlasting
love. All He asks of us is that we respond to Him
with the free will that He has given to us.

NANCIE CARMICHAEL

God's real love becomes more
than a covering cloak.
It saturates our every cell.

ROSE GOBLE

There is unspeakable beauty in brokenness.
Jesus, the Son of God, was broken and His blood
spilled to secure our hope, our future glory.
He was allowed to suffer so that He could offer us
a life of eternal beauty. May we look to Him as our
example when things come along to break us....
May we accept them as gifts of grace,
pieces of the puzzle of our life that will one day
fit together into something beautiful.

GWEN FORD FAULKENBERRY

The Burial of Jesus

Now there was a man named Joseph, a member of the Council, a good and upright man, who had not consented to their decision and action. He came from the Judean town of Arimathea, and he himself was waiting for the kingdom of God. Going to Pilate, he asked for Jesus' body. Then he took it down, wrapped it in linen cloth and placed it in a tomb cut in the rock, one in which no one had yet been laid. It was Preparation Day, and the Sabbath was about to begin. The women who had come with Jesus from Galilee followed Joseph and saw the tomb and how his body was laid in it. Then they went home and prepared spices and perfumes. But they rested on the Sabbath in obedience to the commandment.

LUKE 23:50–56 NIV

His Sacrifice

*I*n His death Jesus demonstrated God's love
for us in the fullest possible way, achieved total
victory over evil, and made our salvation possible.
He was not merely a good man who died as
an example of virtue or meekness; He was the
perfect God who took our burdens of sin and guilt
and made them His burden. His death was not an
example to inspire us but a sacrifice to save us!

ROD BENSON

*W*e are forgiven and righteous because of
Christ's sacrifice; therefore we are pleasing to God
in spite of our failures. Christ alone is the source
of our forgiveness, freedom, joy, and purpose.

ROBERT S. MCGEE

$\mathcal{G}$od presented Jesus as the sacrifice for sin. People are made right with God when they believe that Jesus sacrificed his life, shedding his blood.... God did this to demonstrate his righteousness, for he himself is fair and just, and he declares sinners to be right in his sight when they believe in Jesus.

ROMANS 3:25–26 NLT

$\mathcal{T}$he cross did what man could not do. It granted us the right to talk with, love, and even live with God.

MAX LUCADO

Infinite Love

An infinite God can give all of Himself to each of His children. He does not distribute Himself that each may have a part, but to each one He gives all of Himself as fully as if there were no others.... His love has not changed. It hasn't cooled off, and it needs no increase because He has already loved us with infinite love and there is no way that infinitude can be increased.... He is the same yesterday, today, and forever!

A. W. TOZER

Infinite and yet personal, personal and yet infinite, God may be trusted because He is the True One. He is true, He acts truly, and He speaks truly.... God's truthfulness is therefore foundational for His trustworthiness.

OS GUINNESS

Christ did not die for people because they were intrinsically worth dying for, but because He is intrinsically love, and therefore loves infinitely.

C. S. Lewis

At the very heart and foundation
of all God's dealings with us, however dark
and mysterious they may be, we must dare
to believe in and assert the infinite, unmerited,
and unchanging love of God.

L. B. Cowman

*I've loved you the way my Father has loved
me. Make yourselves at home in my love.*

John 15:9 MSG

Amazing Grace

This is the amazing story of God's grace.
God saves us by His grace and transforms us
more and more into the likeness of His Son
by His grace. In all our trials and afflictions, He
sustains and strengthens us by His grace. He calls
us by grace to perform our own unique function
within the Body of Christ. Then, again by grace,
He gives to each of us the spiritual gifts necessary
to fulfill our calling. As we serve Him, He makes
that service acceptable to Himself by grace, and
then rewards us a hundredfold by grace.

JERRY BRIDGES

After winter comes the summer.
After night comes the dawn. And after every
storm, there comes clear, open skies.

SAMUEL RUTHERFORD

God has not promised skies always blue,
flower-strewn pathways all our lives through;
God has not promised sun without rain,
joy without sorrow, peace without pain.
But God has promised strength for the day,
rest for the labor, light for the way,
grace for the trials, help from above,
unfailing sympathy, undying love.

ANNIE JOHNSON FLINT

Behold, God is my helper;
the Lord is the sustainer of my soul.

PSALM 54:4 NASB

New Dimensions

*G*od raised up Jesus, not simply to give
credence to man's immemorial hopes of life
beyond the grave, but to shatter history
and remake it by a cosmic,
creative event, ushering in a new age
and a new dimension of existence.

JAMES S. STEWART

I ask...that with both feet planted firmly on
love, you'll be able to take in with all followers of
Jesus the extravagant dimensions of Christ's love.
Reach out and experience the breadth!
Test its length! Plumb the depths! Rise to the
heights! Live full lives, full in the fullness of God.

EPHESIANS 3:16–19 MSG

Calvary is a telescope through which we look into the long vista of eternity and see the love of God breaking forth into time.

MARTIN LUTHER KING JR.

The Breadth: "For God so loved the world"
The Length: "that He gave His only begotten Son"
The Depth: "that whoever believes in Him
shall not perish"
The Height: "but have everlasting life."

*Easter is the demonstration of God
that life is essentially spiritual and timeless.*

CHARLES M. CROWE

Resurrection

For if we have been united with him
in a death like his, we will certainly also be
united with him in a resurrection like his.
For we know that our old self was crucified with
him so that the body ruled by sin might be done
away with, that we should no longer be slaves to
sin—because anyone who has died has been set
free from sin. Now if we died with Christ,
we believe that we will also live with him.

ROMANS 6:5–8 NIV

Let the resurrection joy lift us from
loneliness and weakness and despair
to strength and beauty and happiness.

FLOYD W. TOMKINS

The day of resurrection, Earth tell it out abroad!
The Passover of gladness, the Passover of God.
From death to life eternal,
from this world to the sky,
Our Christ has brought us over,
with hymns of victory.

JOHN OF DAMASCUS

I marvel at the way
That hope keeps breaking through;
It is the Life in me
That keeps on reenacting
Resurrection.

GLORIA GAITHER

Oh, Glorious, Merciful, Omnipotent God!
He is risen indeed!... Christ, our Lord, is faithful to
His promises. If you're not presently "seeing" Him at
work in your situation, do not live as if He's lifeless
and you're hopeless. Believe Him and expect Him
to reveal His resurrection power to you!

BETH MOORE

He Is Risen!

$Very$ early on Sunday morning the women went to the tomb, taking the spices they had prepared. They found that the stone had been rolled away from the entrance. So they went in, but they didn't find the body of the Lord Jesus. As they stood there puzzled, two men suddenly appeared to them, clothed in dazzling robes. The women were terrified and bowed with their faces to the ground. Then the men asked, "Why are you looking among the dead for someone who is alive? He isn't here! He is risen from the dead!..." So they rushed back from the tomb to tell his eleven disciples—and everyone else—what had happened.

LUKE 24:1–6, 9 NLT

Dawn of a New Day

Early on Sunday morning, as the new day was dawning, Mary Magdalene and the other Mary went out to visit the tomb. Suddenly there was a great earthquake! For an angel of the Lord came down from heaven, rolled aside the stone, and sat on it. His face shone like lightning, and his clothing was as white as snow. The guards shook with fear when they saw him, and they fell into a dead faint. Then the angel spoke to the women. "Don't be afraid!" he said. "I know you are looking for Jesus, who was crucified. He isn't here! He is risen from the dead, just as he said would happen."

MATTHEW 28:1–6 NLT

*W*hen you feel in your own heart the
suffering of Christ, remember the resurrection
has to come, the joy of Easter has to dawn.

MOTHER TERESA

*E*aster is a day to fan the ashes of dead hope,
a day to banish doubts and seek the slopes
where the sun is rising, to revel in the faith
which transports us out of ourselves and the
dead past into the vast and inviting unknown.

*C*hrist has turned all
of our sunsets into dawns.

CLEMENT OF ALEXANDRIA

Power to Live

Jesus Himself conquered death,
hell, and the grave. Nothing could hold
Him down. He rose from the grave
on that third victorious day.
And now that same power that
raised Jesus from the dead, lives in us!
We don't have to be chained to sin
and death any longer.

MICHAEL NEALE

If the Spirit of him who raised Jesus
from the dead is living in you,
he who raised Christ from the dead
will also give life to your mortal bodies
because of his Spirit who lives in you.

ROMANS 8:11 NIV

Life from the Center is a life of unhurried
peace and power. It is simple. It is serene....
We need not get frantic. He is at the helm.

THOMAS R. KELLY

Do not pray for easy lives. Pray to be stronger.
Do not pray for tasks equal to your powers.
Pray for powers equal to your tasks.
Then the doing of your work shall be no miracle,
but you shall be the miracle.

PHILLIPS BROOKS

*The Creator of all thinks enough of you
to have sent Someone very special so that
you might have life—abundantly, joyfully,
completely, and victoriously.*

Victorious Day!

Tomb, thou shalt not hold Him longer;
Death is strong, but Life is stronger;
Stronger than the dark, the light;
Stronger than the wrong, the right;
Faith and Hope triumphant say
Christ will rise on Easter Day.

PHILLIPS BROOKS

When the perishable has been clothed with the
imperishable, and the mortal with immortality,
then the saying that is written will come true:
"Death has been swallowed up in victory."
"Where, O death, is your victory?
Where, O death, is your sting?"

1 CORINTHIANS 15:54–55 NIV

*I*f Easter says anything to us today, it says this: You can put truth in a grave, but it won't stay there. You can nail it to a cross, wrap it in winding sheets, and shut it up in a tomb, but it will rise!

CLARENCE W. HALL

*A*ngels, roll the rock away;
Death, yield up thy mighty prey:
See, He rises from the tomb,
Glowing with immortal bloom.

THOMAS SCOTT

*I am the resurrection and the life.
The one who believes in me will live,
even though they die; and whoever lives
by believing in me will never die.*

JOHN 11:25–26 NIV

Our Alleluia!

The yes of Easter is the most welcome word
we hear all year. It is our alleluia.

CHERYL FORBES

Hallelujah! I give thanks to GOD
with everything I've got—
Wherever good people gather,
and in the congregation.
God's works are so great, worth
A lifetime of study—endless enjoyment!
Splendor and beauty mark his craft;
His generosity never gives out.
His miracles are his memorial—
This GOD of Grace, this God of Love.
He gave food to those who fear him,
He remembered to keep his ancient promise.
He proved to his people that he could do
what he said....

He manufactures truth and justice;
All his products are guaranteed to last—
Never out-of-date, never obsolete, rust-proof.
All that he makes and does is honest and true:
He paid the ransom for his people,
He ordered his Covenant kept forever.
He's so personal and holy, worthy of our respect.
The good life begins in the fear of GOD—
Do that and you'll know the blessing of GOD.
His Hallelujah lasts forever!

PSALM 111:1–3 MSG

The strife is over, the battle done;
The victory of life is won.
The song of triumph has begun,
O sing "Alleluia!"

I Will Arise

Let every man and woman count themselves immortal. Let them catch the revelation of Jesus in His resurrection. Let them say not merely, "Christ is risen," but "I shall rise."

PHILLIPS BROOKS

Celestial spirit that does roll
The heart's sorrowful stone away,
Be this our resurrection day,
The singing Easter of the soul—
O gentle Master of the Wise,
Teach us to say: "I will arise."

RICHARD LE GALLIENNE

The cross is the only ladder high enough
to touch the threshold of heaven.

GEORGE DANA BOARDMAN

*P*raise be to the God and Father of our Lord Jesus Christ! In his great mercy he has given us new birth into a living hope through the resurrection of Jesus Christ from the dead, and into an inheritance that can never perish, spoil or fade. This inheritance is kept in heaven for you.

1 PETER 1:3–4 NIV

*S*oar we now where Christ has led; Alleluia!
Following our exalted Head; Alleluia!
Made like Him, like Him we rise; Alleluia!
Ours the cross, the grave, the skies. Alleluia!

CHARLES WESLEY

*In the resurrection of Christ
we foresee our own resurrection.*

ALBERTA DANNER

As a Matter of Fact

The work of Christ is a fact, His cross is a fact,
His tomb is a fact, His resurrection is a fact. You
are not called upon to believe something that is
not credible, but to believe in the fact of history.

BILLY GRAHAM

We are not saved by theories, but by fact,
and what is the fact? For whom did Christ die?
Christ died for sinners. Well, then, He died for me.

ARTHUR STANTON

The fundamental fact of existence is that this
trust in God, this faith, is the firm foundation
under everything that makes life worth living.

HEBREWS 11:1–2 MSG

The fact that Jesus came to earth where he suffered and died does not remove pain from our lives. But it does show that God did not sit idly by and watch us suffer in isolation. God became one of us.... *How does God feel about our pain?* In reply, God did not give us words or theories on the problem of pain. God gave us himself.

Philip Yancey

The essential fact of Easter is that God thought all people worth the sacrifice of His Son.

William Barclay

An Invitation

If you have ever:

   questioned if this is all there is to life...

   wondered what happens when you die...

   felt a longing for purpose or significance...

   wrestled with resurfacing anger...

   struggled to forgive someone...

   known there is a "higher power" but

      couldn't define it...

   sensed you have a role to play in the world...

   experienced success and still felt empty afterward...

then consider Jesus.

A great teacher from two millennia ago, Jesus of Nazareth, freely chose to show our Maker's everlasting love for us by offering to take all of our flaws, darkness, and mistakes into His very body (1 Peter 2:24). The result was His death on a cross. But the story doesn't end there. God raised Him to newness of life, and invites us to believe this truth in our hearts and follow Jesus into eternal life.

If you confess with your mouth that Jesus is Lord and believe in your heart that God raised him from the dead, you will be saved. –ROMANS 10:9